What Do We Know About
GRASSLANDS?

PETER BEDRICK BOOKS
NEW YORK

First American Edition published in 1992 by
Peter Bedrick Books
2112 Broadway
New York, NY 10023

Copyright © 1991 by Simon & Schuster
Young Books

Published by agreement with Simon & Schuster Young
Books, Hemel Hempstead, England

Author Dr. Brian Knapp
Art Director Duncan McCrae
Illustrator Mark Franklin
Designed and produced by
EARTHSCAPE EDITIONS
Printed and bound in Hong Kong

Library of Congress Cataloguing-in-Publication Data

Knapp, Brian J.
  What do we know about Grasslands? (Caring for environme
  Brian Knapp. — 1st American ed.
  Includes index.
  Summary: A geographic survey of the earth's
  grasslands, their climate and ecological importance.
  ISBN 0-87226-359-2
  1. Grasslands--Juvenile literature. 2. Grasslands
  ecology--Juvenile literature. 3. Range management
  --Juvenile literature. 4. Man -- Influence on nature
  --Juvenile literature. [1. Grasslands. 2. Praries.
  3. Savannas.] I. Title. II. Series
  QH541.5.P7K53 1992
  574.5'2643--dc20   92-7888
                                                         CIP
                                                          AC

Picture credits

        t=top b=bottom l=left r=right

All photographs from the Earthscape Editions
photographic library except the following:
Colorific – Front Cover, 27b; ZEFA – 10/11,
21t, 24t, 24/25, 25r

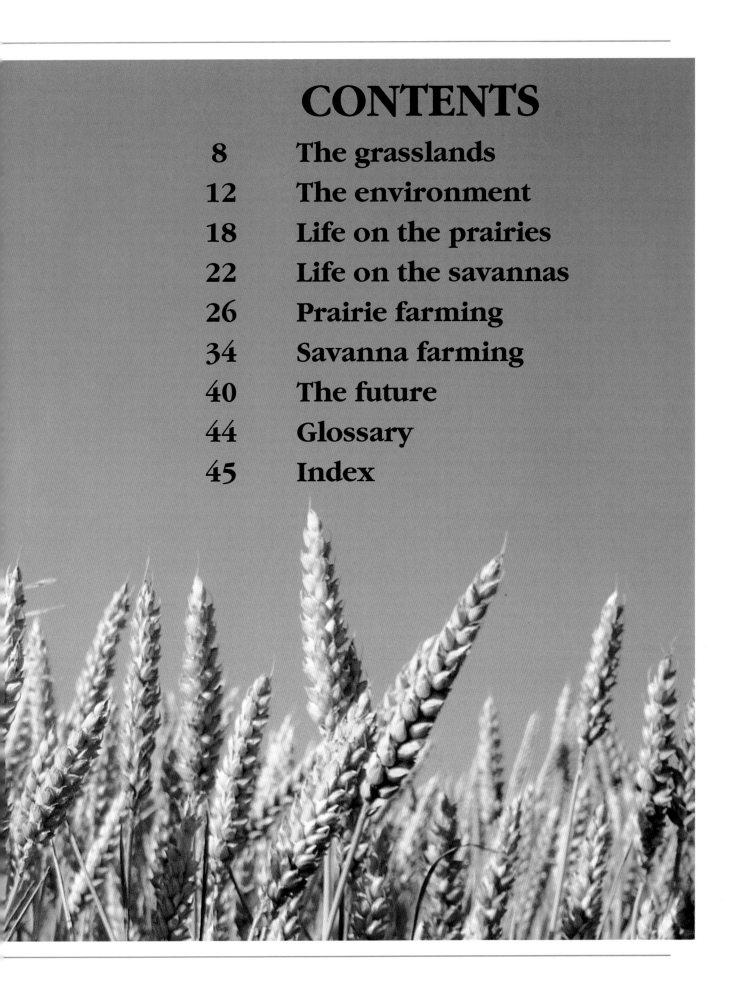

CONTENTS

1: THE GRASSLANDS

Grasslands – places where trees are rare and where vast herds of grazing animals once made their homes – make up over a quarter of the earth's surface. They lie either side of the great deserts of the world, often at the heart of continents, clothing seemingly unbroken plains.

Grasslands are places of great beauty for those with the time to look, and of greater wealth for those who treasure the land. Yet they have witnessed some of the greatest man-made disasters and almost unparalleled tragedies that can be found anywhere in the world.

The map shows the parts of the world that are climatically suited to be grasslands. Inside the tropics such grasslands are called savannas. In the temperate zones they are called prairies. However, farmers have used most of the natural grasslands for grazing or cultivation, and little natural vegetation survives.

Lands of extremes

Perhaps surprisingly for land that sounds as though it is home to no more than 'grass', the grasslands are places of immense variety. Because the two great belts of grassland are isolated by impenetrable deserts, each has evolved quite differently. Nevertheless, the long dry periods provide a common thread, because they can be tolerated by grasses but are more than most trees can withstand.

The grasslands nearest the Equator (the tropical grasslands) are hot throughout the year. They are commonly called **savannas**. They have one or two long dry seasons separated by wet seasons – periods with torrential rain.

By contrast, the grasslands on the poleward side of the deserts (the temperate grasslands, which we shall call **prairies** for short) have hot and cold seasons. Their droughts are brought about by long periods when the ground is frozen and snow-covered, and a summer where rain from thunderstorms rarely sinks deeply into the ground.

These differences in climate have affected the soils and the way nature has adapted to its environment. The savanna is naturally far more productive than the prairie, although that is not always the way people have perceived it, as we shall see later.

The prairies are most famous for native peoples such as the North American Indians. Only some types of Indians lived on the Prairies. Their temporary homes – tepees – speak of the nomadic ways forced on these people as they followed the herds in their annual migrations, in search of fresh pasture.

Tropic of Cancer

Equator

Tropic of Capricorn

Grasslands

Where mistakes cost dear

Prairies and savannas have been but thinly populated for most of their history. Although the land was well provided with animals, it did not prove easy for people to survive, partly because of the weather, but also because these are fragile lands, and their natural balance is easily upset.

Fire has been the age-old tool of the people of these areas. Through their use of fire, people have probably increased the land that is called grassland far beyond its natural boundaries. And as people burned back the forest margin, so they opened the land to the herds who, through their grazing habits, made sure that new saplings never had a chance to re-establish themselves.

But the grasslands themselves have been under increasing stress. The prairies were the first to be altered as wave after wave of settlers arrived to seek their fortunes. By the beginning of this century many prairie lands were hardly recognizable when compared with half a century earlier. In the second part of the twentieth century it has been the savannas which have been attacked, 'nibbled at the edges', by millions of people in search of a place to call home and land to work.

The wide open plains of the savannas are interrupted by occasional hills known as inselbergs. These are the remains of even higher plains, long since eroded.

Savannas are often called savanna parkland, a reference back to eighteenth century Britain, when it was fashionable for a large estate to be laid out with broad areas of grass and the occasional tree. But it is a useful reminder that, unlike the prairies, where trees cannot survive, savannas can support both trees and grasses. The main tree in this picture is an **acacia**.

The traditional people of the savanna have close ties with the land. The Aborigines of northwest Australia and nomadic hunters of East Africa, such as the Masai shown in this picture, are the tropical grassland equivalent of the North American Indians. Each group learned through experience how to gain a living from a difficult environment.

2: THE ENVIRONMENT

The grasslands are lands of transition. Just as a child inherits some characteristics from both parents, so the grasslands, which lie between **humid** and **arid** regions, pick up some of the characteristics of both types of climate.

Seasonal changes in the grasslands' weather. *The diagram below shows the weather experienced by the prairies and savannas in January. By July the overhead sun has moved north of the equator and the pattern is reversed.*

Seasons of the savanna

The savannas lie between the barren deserts and the tropical rainforests that cloak the regions near the Equator. Here the weather changes with the movement of the overhead sun. For part of the year – the dry season – the overhead sun is far away, and hot scorching winds from the deserts blow over the land, withering all but the most hardy plants and animals. This is a time when the land is tinder-dry and can easily be set ablaze.

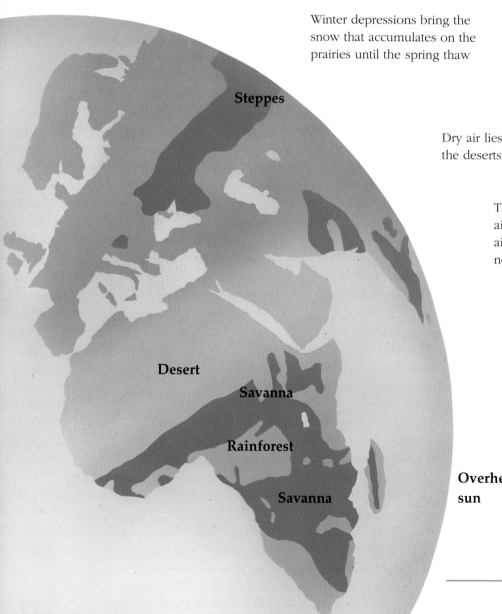

Winter depressions bring the snow that accumulates on the prairies until the spring thaw

Steppes

Dry air lies over the deserts

The warm, moist equatorial air retreats and the dry desert air advances to give the northern savanna dry season

Tropical rainforests lie near the equator where rising air causes thunderstorms through the year

Desert

Savanna

Rainforest

Savanna

Overhead sun

The warm, moist equatorial air advances southward bringing moisture for the southern savanna rainy season

Then, as the months go by and the sun moves more closely overhead, the desert influence wanes and is replaced by hot humid winds carrying moisture brought from the oceans. This signals the onset of the rainy season and, strangely, the time of greatest danger of all. Each day the clouds form and get a little thicker and a little darker, but no rain falls. Then one day the clouds are thick enough for lightning to form. This is the time when sparks jump between layers of the clouds and between the clouds and the ground. A spark striking the ground will quickly set the dry grass alight, only to be fanned by the winds that accompany each thundercloud.

Fire may affect the savanna for days or weeks before the parched land becomes drenched by the first of the rainy season storms. Temperatures fall and huge drops of rain pound down on the soil, quickly forming sheets of water that follow every small dip in the land until they gather to make surging, mud-filled rivers. In some places the beginning of the rains is very marked indeed, and in such places the rainy season is called the **monsoon**.

The rainy season begins dramatically but ends quietly a month or two later. Each day a little less rain falls, until there are more dry days than rainy ones. Eventually the clouds evaporate in the sky before they can produce rain and the land begins to dry out rapidly. The dry season has returned, but now the sun shines over lands that have been transformed from brown and parched wilderness to lands rich in green grasses.

Prairie extremes

If the main feature of a savanna is its pattern of wet and dry seasons, so the

Boiling up into the sky, this thunderstorm *may release several inches of rain in a few minutes. Thunderstorms form in the mid-day sun and bring violent storms during the late afternoon.*

Thunderstorms are important for the rain they bring, but also for the fires that their lightning causes.

main feature of a prairie is its staggering shift from intense cold to stifling heat. A swing from -4°F in mid-winter to +86°F in mid-summer is not uncommon. The people who live on the prairies say it is the weather that keeps the less hardy people out. This is because the plains experience greater weather extremes than anywhere else in the world.

Only the continental heartlands, or areas in the lee of great mountain ranges, produce climates with great weather extremes. In the winter, continents cool down and cool the air that lies above them. The cold, and therefore dense and heavy, air then settles down on the land like a huge blanket. It is called a high pressure region.

The winter high pressure is very powerful. It steers all the rain-bearing winds around its edge, so that clouds and storms are rare. Those that do get to the plains bring only brief snowstorms. Winters are therefore bright and sunny, but very cold. With the landscape offering so little shelter, winds constantly blow, bringing a chill to the land that only the most hardy plants and wildlife can withstand.

The first thunderstorms often set the grasslands alight. How much damage is done depends on the time since the last burn. If there has been a long interval, the dry growth will burn fiercely, as in the picture above. If the interval has been short, fire will simply speed across the land, merely singing the vegetation and turning dead litter into useful ash, as shown in the picture on the right.

Savanna soils are closely linked with the climate. *A long dry season offers little opportunity for dead plant matter to rot down as it would in more humid regions. Soils in the savanna tend to be sandy and dusty.*

Rotted material is the key to life in a soil. Even tiny amounts of decayed organic matter – humus – will provide the long sticky threads that can bind soil particles and hold them fast against rain or wind. In an area with little humus, an exposed soil is very vulnerable indeed, and when left exposed it is quickly washed or blown away.

The main soil creatures are termites. Only a few millimeters long, these white-bodied, ant-like creatures live in immense colonies partly below the surface. They build immense structures to live in called termitariums. These mud castles have tall chimneys which act as ventilation shafts. As they build their nests, so they bring material from two metres or more below the ground and pile it on the surface. In this way they turn the soil over, helping to enrich it.

Each year termites turn over many tons of soil per acre. But there is a vast army of other burrowing animals which tunnel about looking for roots to eat. They, too, play a useful role in aerating the soils and allowing the rains to seep into the ground rather than run over the surface.

Spring is short and swift. The white snow reflects most of the sun's rays and springs are late. It is warm air penetrating from beyond the plains that finally brings an end to winter. Then warm winds feed across the plains and quickly melt the snow. Some of the meltwater sinks into the soil to give life-giving moisture to the plants and seeds. Much of the rest runs off to threaten towns and cities with river floods.

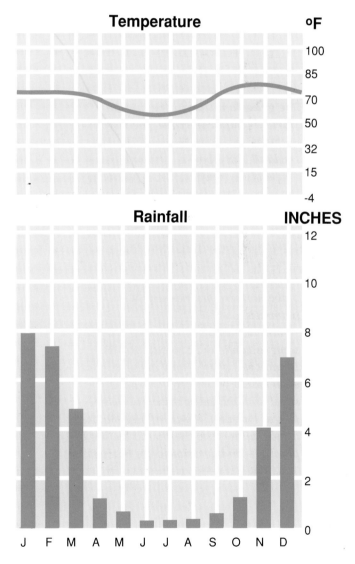

Temperature °F

100
85
70
50
32
15
-4

Rainfall INCHES

12
10
8
6
4
2
0

J F M A M J J A S O N D

The pattern of temperature and rainfall *for Harare, Zimbabwe, southern Africa.*

Spring winds bring moisture, cloud and rain. But the season of rains is quickly over and the searing heat of summer begins. Heating allows the land to develop an intense low pressure region, and this sucks in air from the surrounding regions. Some air streams are very moist and will give rise to thunderstorms. In North America, air sucked into the prairies from the Gulf of Mexico is full of moisture. By contrast, air from the mountains is usually dry and it simply sets up hot winds that scorch the land. Which type of air dominates will decide if a summer is to be dry or wet, but there is no easy way to tell what it will be like in advance.

There is a daily pattern to the summer season weather. The plains heat up quickly each day. The air near the ground becomes warmed and light, and rises to form huge thermals. If there is enough moisture in the air these soon swell into thunderstorms with torrential rain. Thermals in this air bring tornadoes as well as thunderstorms.

Autumn is as brief as spring. The sun no longer causes the thunderstorms and the air become calmer as the first of the frosts begins.

The grasslands lie in the middle of the world's temperate zone, *the zone that includes New York, USA, and London, England. But whereas London has a temperature range of 55° F, Winnipeg – a major Canadian prairie city – has, for example, a yearly range of 100° F. Summer temperatures in Winnipeg and London are hardly different, but whereas London has a mild winter, with a lowest temperature of 41° F, the temperature of the northern prairies near Winnipeg plummets to -4° F.*

Annual rainfall in Winnipeg is about the same as London (22 inches). But whereas London gets nearly equal amounts of rain each month, Winnipeg stores all its winter snow until the spring thaw. Summer rain falls as torrential thunderstorms that may throw hailstones to the ground the size of peaches – and devastate crops in the fields.

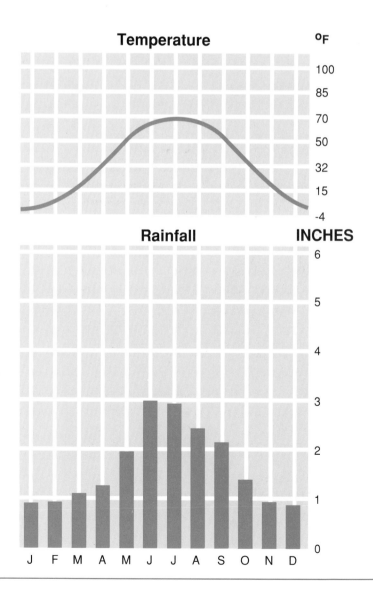

Drought comes in cycles

The grasslands thrive when there is plenty of rain. But if the rains fail there will be drought and great hardship.

Plentiful rains and droughts occur in cycles of about a decade. So for ten years there will be good rains, but in the following ten years there will be many severe droughts, crops will fail, and wildlife will die. It is the cyclic change of rainfall that has always been the curse of the grasslands. Nature and people have tried to deal with it in different ways as we shall see.

The daily thunderstorm cycle forming over part of a short grass prairie.

The black and dark brown soils of the prairies are very different from the red soils of the savannas. Where the savannas develop a strong red-brown colored soil which is dominated by the rusty iron color of the rock, the black color of the prairie soil is a sign of rich humus.

Prairie soils support grasses with deep roots. As we shall see, just like an iceberg, up to nine-tenths of the prairie vegetation may be hidden from view. In this case it is the deep roots that form a dense net in the soil. When they die the roots can be rotted to humus, the cause of the black color.

Some prairie soils are called Chernozems, a word which literally means 'black soil' in Russian. It is the black gold of the farmer, and a soil which can support some of the most intense farming in the world. But it is nonetheless fragile. In a natural world the grass roots die and are renewed, thus producing new humus each year.

The picture on the right shows a dark brown Chestnut Soil from the drier prairie. Notice the fine silty material on which the soil has formed. It is easy to plough but is also very prone to erosion if the protective surface vegetation is removed.

3: LIFE ON THE PRAIRIES

urviving on the prairies is no easy matter. There is heat, drought and cold with which to contend as well as the constant threat of predators. The difficulties of survival have driven much of the natural world underground, so a prairie is a place where you have to look hard to understand its way of life.

Plants equipped to survive

Plants have to brave all these weather extremes. They cannot move from the place where they have started to grow, so it is vital that they can survive all but the most ferocious onslaught by the weather. This is why the fronds of grasses you see on a prairie are just a small part of the total plant: most of it lies buried deep within the ground.

Prairie grasses are called 'tussock' grasses because they branch out from a compact root stock. The new growth is protected from summer range fires, hidden away in the center of the tussock. By being larger, the plant can also grow long roots which will reach water in all but the driest season.

Grasses that have to survive heat and drought cannot have thick fleshy blades waving in the wind. Instead they must be tough and wiry. Many are needle shaped, not only to reduce their loss of moisture, but also because this shape will best withstand the strong winds that frequently blow over the plains.

Moisture is such a precious commodity that plants share it in special ways. There are some plants that grow very slowly, but steadily, all summer. Then there are others that grow quickly just after the spring rains, flowering and producing seed within a couple of months. These tend to be varieties that have roots that seek water near the surface. And finally there are plants that only begin their growth when the early plants have already flowered and have fewer demands for water. These plants have the deepest rooting systems, searching down for the moisture that lies well below the surface.

Just over a century ago, the land rang to the thunder of the hooves of millions of **herbivores**, like the bison, and was dotted with many flowering herbs. Since then people have thoughtlessly exterminated the majority of the bison and used herbicides on the flowers. Today just a few small herds, like the one shown in this picture, remain to give a flavour of the past. Flowering plants, like those in the inset picture, are just as elusive.

Bison have thick coats which they need to keep warm through the savage winter. They are shed in summer, giving the animals a rather ragged appearance.

Animals without number

Prairies are the natural home to a very large number of animals, but as on the savannas, these animals are in balance with both the plants they eat and the predators that hunt them.

When people think of the natural prairies, they often think of the huge herds of hoofed animals that once ranged freely across the plains. Each continent has its own range of species, but each species has its equivalent in the other continents.

The main grazers are very selective in their choice of food. This is the reason why many species could graze together. It is only in a drought that competition for the scarce grazing becomes severe.

The **predators**, animals like bears and packs of wolves or solitary eagles and owls, are less obvious. Without cover of trees many of them hunt by night and take shelter in holes by day. Even eagles and owls, whose perches are naturally on branches above the ground, have adapted to living on the ground, and in the case of the owl, even nesting in a burrow.

Keeping out of trouble

The herd of grazers defends itself by running away and by the sheer weight of its numbers. A fully grown antelope will turn on a wolf or a bear. It is the old, the young, and the infirm that mostly fall prey to the hunters.

The smaller animals cannot outrun a predator and their strategy must be different. One of the most common small animals is the ground squirrel, a rodent commonly called a prairie dog. This animal lives in complex network of tunnels about 2 feet below the surface. It is a very communal creature

A coyote makes the most of a meal on a carcass of an antelope during the fierce prairie winter.

A prairie dog stands upright with ears pricked, listening and watching for signs of danger. These rodents use the ground for protection from the weather as well as from predators.

and lives with many hundreds of others in a community called a prairie dog town.

The tunnels have many uses. A prairie dog can scavenge for plant roots, seeds and insects near to its tunnel, then dart into safety if it sees a predator approaching. It is also a good place to hibernate. **Hibernation** is important because the ground is snow-covered and frozen hard for several winter months. Being below the ground, the prairie dog can use the soil as an insulating blanket.

4: LIFE ON THE SAVANNAS

If plants are to survive on a savanna they must be adapted to heat, drought and fire. Heat can scorch leaves and cause wilting even when the soil still has moisture in it; drought can drain all the moisture from the soil, leaving plants to die; and fire can scorch the leaves and shooting buds.

Stubborn grasses

To cope with all these problems plants have to be sturdy and to have many defences. For example, the savanna 'elephant' grasses may reach 10 or more feet when they are fully grown in the wet season, but the roots stretch just as far below the surface as the stems reach above it. You would not succeed in pulling a savanna grass up by the roots

An acacia on fire; only the outer branches are singed during burning.

Acacia thorns are needle sharp and very tough. The thorns are hollow to give them extra strength. The thorn shown below is life size.

in the same way you would a grass from a humid area.

In the dry season, when the wiry stems and leaves of the grasses die back to conserve moisture, the roots make up over nine-tenths of the mass of grass. But deep roots that can search out moisture even in the depth of drought are not the only way grasses survive. Savanna grasses are tussock grasses, which means they have many stems branching out from a single root mass, or tussock. This means that all savanna grasses are substantial plants, and if fire sweeps across the land, buds set deep within the tussock have a much better chance of survival than single exposed grasses.

Tough trees

Trees have to be even more hardy than grasses, because they cannot die back in the dry season and take shelter from fire in the ground. Trees have to cope by growing thick scales on their buds, and tucking the buds into well protected sites in crooks between branches and twigs. And if the worst comes to the worst and the tree catches fire, many species have buds on their roots which will spring into life after the fire has gone away and the rains come again.

Savanna grasses grow vigorously during the rainy season and often reach several yards in height.

Tree survival in a land of grass

Parched lands are not easy places for trees. Only two species of tree commonly dot the savanna grasslands. The most frequent is the group of flat crowned trees known as acacias.

Acacias are modestly sized trees, growing to only 33 feet in height and having trunks less than a yard across. Acacia branches are armed with long thorns – like the ones shown on the opposite page – which defeat some browsers, although not the specialized feeders like the giraffe. To protect themselves against the long dry season, many acacias are deciduous and shed their leaves as the drought bites. They also have very deep roots so that they can make the most of the moisture stored in the soil after the rainy season.

The other common group of trees found in savanna regions is the baobab, or boab, found in Australia. It is sometimes called the 'upside down' tree because in the dry season when it sheds its leaves, its stumpy and ungainly branches look a little like roots sticking up the air.

The seed of the baobab protects itself from animals by being as hard as a rock. Yet its case will soften and produce shoots at the onset of the rains.

Many savanna trees are very slow-growing, but the baobab is one of the slowest of all. The one shown in the picture below may be a thousand years old. Mature trees reach 66 feet high with a trunk diameter of up to 10 feet.

The baobab saves water in two ways: first, like the acacia, by shedding its leaves in the dry seasons; second, by storing water in its thick pulpy trunk.

This is a baobab tree during the dry season. Its short stumpy branches are an indication that it grows very slowly. It becomes covered in an irregular foliage of dark green leaves during the wet season.

Savanna animals

The natural savanna is a place of great contrasts. It contains some of the world's fastest, largest and most ferocious animals. But no matter how large or small, fast or slow, ferocious or timid, each animal depends on others and on the savanna grasses and trees. This is called a **food chain**.

The animals that depend directly on the growing plants are called herbivores. In the savanna the grazing herbivores are often easy to spot because they move in vast herds for protection. The most

The natural savanna is home to huge herds *of herbivores like the wildebeest seen in the picture below. The young, old and infirm fall prey to the hunters, like cheetahs shown on the left.*

In the savanna, rainfall varies greatly from year to year. In rainy years grasses grow strongly and there is plenty for the grazers. In a drought year many animals starve. The number of hunters changes in a similar way.

common herds contain zebra, antelope, buffalo, gazelle and wildebeest. They keep on the move, continually searching for morsels of fresh grass.

Not all the herbivores eat grass. Some – the taller or more agile animals like the giraffe and elephant – eat the leaves from thorn trees or bushes. These **browsers** are smaller in numbers simply because trees are less common on the savanna. Many of the most spectacular savanna animals are the hunters, or **carnivores**.

The large cats like the lion, cheetah and leopard use speed or surprise to catch their prey. In the air the hunters are the eagles, and their prey consists of small ground animals, like the hyrax.

Like all the creatures of the savanna, the large animals depend on each other: the grazing herds turn grass into meat which in turn becomes food for the hunters. In time the grazers and the hunters die and become the food for the **decomposers** – mostly insects – which turn carcasses back into nutrients that the plants can use to grow again. In this way life in the savannas is a cycle in balance. This is nature's way of keeping a balance, but all can be disrupted by the appearance of people.

Elephants are the savannas' largest creatures. A bull African elephant can weight 7.5 tons and have tusks 10 feet long. It can also eat its way through over 300 pounds of leaves a day, so it needs plenty of space to survive.

It uses its long trunk to haul down branches as well as to suck water from pools.

5: PRAIRIE FARMING

If you were to have taken a wagon and horses and gone westwards from the Midwest town of Chicago in the early part of the last century, you would have seen the North American grasslands looking much as they had done for thousands of years. You would slowly have moved across huge plains, waist-high in grasses and flowers. From time to time you would have come across enormous herds of great, shaggy grazing animals – the bison – or equally large herds of antelope. Perhaps you would also have caught sight of hyenas and bears.

To the untrained eyes of the first European explorers, the prairies seemed monotonous plains containing endless tracts of equally monotonous grasses – almost a wasteland. This impression is conveyed vividly in their reports:

Two of the most important changes *to affect the prairies were the destruction of the bison and other large grazing animals, and, later, the planting of wheat and other cereals.*

The picture above shows 'Buffalo Bill', William Cody, famous among the nineteenth century hunters who indiscriminately slaughtered the wildlife. At the time it was seen as man against nature, a matter of survival. Today many people are convinced that the whole approach was misguided.

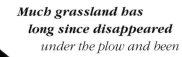

Much grassland has long since disappeared *under the plow and been replaced by productive maize, wheat and barley. Now the natural grasses can only be found in the verges that divide road from field. The first settlers saw the richness of the land, but they failed to understand that the richness was the result of thousands of years of activity by wildlife. When they eliminated the wildlife they lost the source of the richness and now the fertility has to be achieved by using artificial fertilizers.*

Cattle now graze only on the drier ranges of the prairies. One cow to about 5 acres is the highest density of stock that can safely be grazed on dry prairies without overgrazing.

Before scientists studied the problem of overgrazing, many prairie areas were ruined and the ground had been laid bare to erosion.

'As far as the eye could reach in every direction there was neither tree nor shrub, nor house nor shed visible . . . '

' When we were told of these treeless lands I imagined it was a country ravaged by fire and so poor that it could produce nothing.'

'This country (the high western prairies of North America) may be termed the "Desert of America" as I do not conceive any part could ever be settled.'

The lands of the prairies have been depicted in a thousand movies as dry lands, where cattle must be given large areas on which to find enough food. The original farmers were ranchers who used to run cattle together on the range, branding them so they could be identified at the time of sale.

Water is the key to successful rangeland farming, and the rights to gain access to the few rivers for watering cattle were jealously guarded. When sheep were introduced to the range, their ability to eat grass below the feeding height for cattle led to the cattle wars in North America. When the range was finally fenced in, only those with access to water could survive, and the number of ranchers dwindled rapidly.

Rich land, fragile land

Some of the later people to venture into the prairies recognized quite different signs as they read the land. They began to appreciate just how rich this natural world really was.

Their main interest was for farm land. The French (who used to own much of central North America) compared plains grasslands with the grassy (wetter) areas they knew at home. It was they who coined the term 'prairie', which is the French for 'meadowlands'.

Meadows could be used for grazing animals and producing beef. It seemed a shocking waste to allow wild animals to graze where domestic herds could be fattened. And so began the gradual colonization of the prairies, first for cattle, then sheep, and later corn.

For those who knew a good soil, there was no hiding the possibility of developing the land, and within a few decades of the first ranchers establishing their claims, vast tracts had been transformed into areas of high productivity whose surplus crops have earned them the title 'bread basket of the world'.

This picture shows a prairie farm set among wheatfields. In the center the farm buildings house the large machines that are used to manage the land. The towers are silos used to store the harvested grain before it is sent to market. It is a very efficient farming system, but despite all this, the trouble that has to be taken to ensure a good crop can cost more than the crop is worth. Only government subsidies keep most people on this land.

All cereals are now very distant relations to the wild grasses that used to dominate the prairies. These wheat plants have been bred with specially short stems so they are not easily blown over by high winds or knocked down during thunderstorms. They all grow to almost the same height to make it easy for a combined harvester to work quickly, and the ears are far fatter, and ripen more rapidly than any natural grass.

Nevertheless, these 'meadows' are not like European wetland meadows, but fragile dry grasslands which need treating carefully if they – and the people and the wildlife who depend on them – are to survive.

It was this lack of appreciation that caused many great disasters, and none more serious than the loss of soil that gave one area the graphic title, 'the dust bowl'.

Railways change the prairies

The prairies would never have been put under pressure if it had not been for the railways. In the nineteenth century, railway lines were driven across all the world's great prairies.

The railway transformed the accessibility to the prairies. The numbers of grazing animals had previously been restricted by having to take them on long 'cattle drives' of sometimes more than a thousand miles. But the railway meant that a journey of several months could be reduced to several days.

The railway made Chicago in Illinois the beef cattle center of the world, and set the pattern for eating beef that so characterized the American way of life. But it not only made boom cities from towns on the edge of the prairies, it also created boom towns within the prairies. Wherever the railway set up a station, so there existed the chance of getting farm produce to market.

To make all this happen quickly, the railway companies (who owned the land beside the railway) often gave the land away or charged tiny rents. The result was that people arrived in waves. Soon it became clear that the use of land for cattle was not the best way to make a living, and so more and more land went under the plow and a land of grass become a land of corn.

The huge silos that stand beside the railway tracks are a reminder of the importance of good transport to 'opening up' the prairies for intensive farming.

Farming the grasslands has never proved *easy. Poor farmers of the past wrecked the soil and caused erosion. This picture shows an area that was part of the infamous prairie 'dust bowl' of the 1930s as it looks today. You can easily see how dusty the land still is.*

Prairies stretching as far as the eye can see. *It is a fertile land but can only produce crops with huge support from governments.*

The impact of irrigation *can be clearly seen in the picture below. The river is completely dry and the grass range nearby is brown and useless as feed. But a center pivot irrigation well has been used to transform the semicircle of land on the left.*

Irrigation helps many prairie areas to overcome drought problems, but only until the supplies in the rocks deep under the soils are used up. A common means of irrigation is to pump water from the rocks (called aquifers) and then spray it onto the fields using long booms. Some booms travel in a circle, giving this system the title of centered pivot irrigation. They give distinctive patterns form the air, but they are unnoticable from the ground.

Playing with chance

We have described earlier in this book how the climate is made of cycles of well watered years followed by years of drought. It so happened that many of the railways were built across prairies in a time of good rainfall. This, coupled with advertising by the railway, made people think that the prairies were a free paradise. But in fact they were about to play a dangerous game with the land.

The first severe drought hit the North American prairies just at the close of the nineteenth century. Without the aid of wells and means of watering their crops, people were just forced to watch them wither in the fields. The seed they used had not been specially bred to stand up to prairie weather, nor could it make the most of water in the drying soils. But, above all, people had no experience of how to farm these areas. So when the winds blew, as they frequently do across the open prairies, the bare land with its withered crops was simply blown away.

The Dust Bowl

The Dust Bowl is the name given to the part of the North American prairie that centers on the state of Oklahoma. Like other areas, it had been settled by poor people who were making just a bare living at the best of times. The prairies had already shown them that this land was no paradise. The farmers had already survived several droughts and people had little by way of savings to tide them over a bad period. But from the middle of the 1930s onwards there was a very severe drought that proved a disaster not only for the farmers but for the land as well.

So much soil was lost from the surface of the prairies that the air turned yellow and became like a desert dust-storm. Some of the yellow soil was carried as far as the east coast, two thousand miles away. With no money and a soil stripped of much of its fertility many farmers – who became know as 'Okies' after the state which suffered worst – were forced to leave the land. It was the clearest possible signal of the consequences of not caring properly for the environment.

Modern ways

There will be no return to the Dust Bowl because scientists have learned many ways of avoiding a catastrophe in the future. They have shown farmers how to plant a band of corn alternately with a band of grass or some other crop. They have proved to some farmers that they should only plant their land every two years, so that enough moisture can build up in the soil to guarantee a crop. And the farmers themselves have better seed, sturdier crops and equipment, and more government support during bad times. Nobody will take this fragile land for granted again.

Irrigation has been the most important factor in making sure that crops can be helped through a year of drought. The corn growing here (left) is fed by siphons whose arched pipes can be seen leading from the irrigation ditch in the foreground. The crop shown in the picture below is fed from sprinklers.

6: SAVANNA FARMING

Grasses may be food for native wildlife, but they cannot directly make food for people. So it is understandable if people often think of savanna grasslands as wasted land, and decide that it is better used to graze cows or to grow crops.

Many savanna people are not wealthy and own very small parcels of land. So their only way of living is to grow crops to eat. In many cases they are too poor to buy fertilizer and so they must move to new plots when the nutrients in their old plots become used up. This means that a farmer might need twenty times as much land as he cultivates each year.

In the driest regions of the savanna the chances of growing crops successfully are slim and the people rely on cattle, goats or even camels to turn the poor grasslands into meat. Because the land is so poor, each farmer needs a very large area for his animals, and he may need to keep on the move throughout the year if he is to find fresh pasture and save his animals from starvation.

When 100 million families – the present population of the savannas – each cultivate even a small piece of land or each keep just a few animals for grazing, they need to use a large amount of land. Because they are under such pressure to survive themselves, they see wildlife simply as competition for a scarce resource. They are reluctant to see land used for anything else than their food. This is what makes caring for the savanna environment especially difficult.

How savanna life changed

By the end of the nineteenth century the prairies were disappearing fast. But the savannas, which were even more remote and inaccessible to the European farmers, remained largely untouched by outsiders

If you had walked over such land as this with the great explorers – such as David Livingstone – you would have seen a landscape that was a form of fairly open parkland, but with many more trees than you could see today. No matter how inexperienced you might have been, you

Cereals being harvested by hand.

With rapidly expanding populations, much savanna land is under great pressure, and few people have the money to pay for fertilizers. As a result the soil is being 'mined' of its goodness in many areas.

Some savanna regions have a long history of settlement. Most settlement centers on villages, many of them walled or fenced as protection, in part, from wild animals. But these areas are different from the prairies because there is no widespread use of large machines. Much land is still worked by hand. The cereal fields are concentrated near each village with grazing lands beyond. Notice how few trees now dot this landscape. Many have already been used for fuelwood.

could not have failed to notice the rich and varied wildlife. With a single sweep of your eye and a good vantage point you would have been able to see uncountable numbers of grazing animals, wandering over the plains like nomads in a never-ending quest to find young green grass.

Among them you would have seen browsers, such as elephants and giraffes, and the predators, such as the lion and the cheetah. And among these you might have seen some of the nomadic tribespeople whose livelihood matched that of the animals, and from time to time you would have come across a village and its scattering of small fields.

When land is being used for crops there is little left for grazing animals. *Wildlife stands no chance and domestic animals can only survive with the help of people. Here a boy is climbing the remains of a tree to find leaves for his goats.*

This is what happens when savanna land is overused. *The deep gullies were formed when the land was left bare for crops. As the wet season rains poured down the water flowed over the surface until it was powerful enough to tear at the soil and dig deep trenches in the land. Enormous amounts of savanna land have been lost by this kind of erosion.*

Rich land, protected land

It was the parasites, such as the tsetse fly, that kept people at bay for such a long time. While the savanna wildlife has a degree of tolerance to the pests, cattle and people suffer badly, especially from the tsetse fly. Tsetse flies have kept domestic animals from large parts of the savanna to the present day.

Only in the last thirty years has the great explosion of human population, aided by better medicine and nutrition, forced native people to seek to use the savanna more and more. The wetter savannas were turned into farmland long ago, but the drier and more fragile areas are now being put under intolerable pressure.

The new farmers have many parallels to the 'sodbusters' of the prairies. Partly through ignorance, and partly through pressure of circumstance, they have often misused the lands and caused great disasters.

Enormous amounts of water are needed for irrigation because disaster can follow from applying too little irrigation water. This picture shows where too little water has been given to these plants. Instead of draining through the soil and carrying away harmful salts, the heat of the sun has drawn the moisture back to the surface and with it have come salts. With each further inadequate watering more salt is drawn to the surface. The salt is killing these plants.

Hemmed in

In the last century there seemed to be land for all. Those people who lived in the drier areas of the savanna were able to move freely about the countryside, migrating with their animals in search of good grazing. Tribes such as the West African Fulani and the East African Masai became famous nomads, annually migrating right across the savanna between the desert margin and the edge of the rainforest.

As they moved to wetter areas they would bring their cattle to lands that were cultivated by other tribes. Yet there was never any problem because both parties benefited: the cattle would eat any green shoots in land that was not being cultivated, but in exchange they left dung which would provide fertilizer for the next season's crops.

In lands without fertilizers people cannot use the same fields year after year because they soon become infertile. So every few years a farmer will abandon his fields and cultivate some land that has lain fallow. In this way he lets nature make the land fertile again.

This system, called **shifting cultivation**, used to work well when land was plentiful. But as populations have grown, it has proved impossible to leave land fallow for as long as is needed. The farmers have suffered and so have the nomads, for there is no longer any spare land for them to graze. Everyone has become hemmed in to smaller and smaller plots, and they have been forced to work them ever more intensively.

Farming is not the only activity to put pressure on the land. The need to get fuelwood for cooking, for example, has placed enormous burdens on savanna trees. Here a man is putting the finishing touches to a brick kiln. He will bake his bricks with local trees while any remain.

Domestic animals need more water than wild animals. *A farmer has to risk his animals dying in a drought unless he can graze them near to a well.*

The risk business

The people of the savannas largely work the land to survive: they are subsistence farmers. This means that they have to try to choose a strategy that will give them a reliable food supply all year round. Then, if they are lucky, they will have a little left over to sell in the market for luxuries.

This is very different from the prairies, where large scale commercial farmers grow corn for cash. If the crop fails the government will come to their assistance. In the savanna if the crop fails, there is no-one to help and the people might starve. But the crops which grow reliably in the savanna are not necessarily those that are good to eat. It makes farming decisions all the harder.

People like to eat corn but this is not the most reliable crop to grow in many savanna regions. There are several cereals that have been developed from native grasses and which survive in droughts more readily.

The two naturally bred cereals of savanna regions are millet and sorghum. Both crops will give a good yield even in a dry year. They are good at conserving

moisture, so they don't have thick fleshy leaves like maize, and their cereal grains are much smaller and harder. So a farmer must decide on whether to grow some sorghum or millet and have at least some food in a drought year or whether to risk growing maize and have a soft, tasty cereal to eat in rainy years.

If people choose to rear cattle they must be sure that they have a large enough area for grazing, and a reliable supply of water for their animals. Without this they risk starvation.

These children face an uncertain future *if their food supply is not assured. Decisions made by their parents today may make all the difference between a land that is eroded and useless, and a land that can provide all the food they need.*

A hard choice between corn and nature's grass

Savanna grass

For	Against
withstands drought	low nutrient value
resists fire	fibrous and difficult for
binds the soil together	cattle to eat
is not prone to disease	uses most of its growth for roots
grows using the nutrients in the soil	and not leaf

Corn

For	Against
high yield of food	needs fertilizer
can support a family on a small area	needs much attention
uses most energy making leaf	will not withstand drought
animals can be fed leaf and stalk	cannot stand up to fire
	susceptible to disease
	shallow-rooted and does
	not prevent soil erosion

A nursery where new tree seedlings can be grown. The trees can be planted on the terraces. As they grow they will help keep the terraces in place and give fuelwood and fodder for animals.

Learning how to care

The people of the savanna do not like putting too much pressure on their land. They would wish there to be land for wildlife and farmers. But at present there is a danger that there will no land for anyone. The first step must be to care for the soil by digging terraces to stop the water rushing off the land in rainstorms, and to replant trees to combat the spread of gullies. Many people are learning that caring can also be a way of being better off.

The first step to preventing soil erosion is to build terraces across the slopes.
These women are digging terraces. Now, when the rain comes, the water will soak into the soil and be available to crops.

7: THE FUTURE

Savanna and prairie grasslands are places where people and wildlife compete for resources. As we have seen, both kinds of grassland are fragile environments where plants and animals spend all their energies surviving the extremes of the weather. They do not have much resilience to survive the effects of people as well.

Bringing the prairie back to life

After more than a century of intensive farming there is very little land that can still be called prairie in North America. More remains in South America and a little on the Ukranian Steppes. The main thrust of conservation has been to try to find ways of farming that will not destroy the soil completely. Little is done about the natural life because most of it was pushed out long ago.

Yet nature is very resilient and it will recover even from this perilous state with a little help. Traditional ways of using the land, such as can be practiced on Indian reservations where the pressure to farm is less severe, allow some grasses to come back and some rodents and antelopes to return. But this will not easily bring back

Prairies have often been improved by reseeding using grasses that cattle favor. Ranching on natural grasses could allow the prairies to recover.

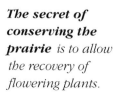

The secret of conserving the prairie is to allow the recovery of flowering plants.

the real prairies because many species lie in such small pockets that they cannot easily spread. What is needed is a continuous tract of land large enough to support a natural community. This is not easy to find because prairie animals need very large areas of land for their survival. Whereas the prairie dogs may colonize a small area, the main grazers, such as the antelope, migrate in search of new shoots. In lands that have been fenced off it is not possible to find a migration route for wild creatures.

Caring for the prairie environment demands drastic measures. Some people have even had to resort to collecting wild prairie grasses by hand and then scattering them again on chosen plots in order to encourage prairies to build up their traditional rich mixture of species. One of the best prairies for plant species is now inside the guarded perimeter of a giant atomic research laboratory called Fermilab in the USA. Here scientists have used the space not occupied by buildings to let a true prairie develop from the seeds that have ben brought to the site.

If there is little room for the traditional prairie, there is even less room for the animals that made it their home. Huge mounds of bison skulls and elk antlers can still be seen as grotesque reminders of the senseless slaughter a century ago. Now the bears and wolves have gone and the magnificent bison are confined, in the most part, to pathetic patches of ground that they overgraze.

The future for the prairie environment looks bleak unless some of the areas in Asia and South America can be held from public pressure, or unless the governments in North America are prepared to buy some of the farmland and let it recover naturally in National Parks.

***The prairies are the breadbaskets of the world.** The USSR gets most of its grain from the Ukraine Steppes. North America exports surpluses to keep the world from hunger. It is unlikely that large areas of the wetter prairies will ever return to grazing land. Caring for the environment here will be a matter of making sure the soil remains healthy and is prevented from blowing or washing away.*

How can the savanna be saved?

The difference between the prairie and the savanna is that, while the prairie farmers have all but destroyed their natural environment, there do still remain unspoiled tracts of savanna. The problem is how to care for them in countries where everyone is desperate for land simply to grow food to eat.

The savannas have been fortunate in coming under pressure only quite recently when much more is known about conservation. But the savannas have a trump card to play – their diversity of wildlife is of considerable attraction to tourists who have the money and the means to visit them. By making large areas into wildlife parks and by encouraging tourists, not only will the animals and plants have a more secure future, but the people in the savanna

countries will have an additional source of income. At the moment they are using up the savanna because they have no other means of survival. Tourist money could be one way of ensuring that the savannas are of more value left alone than they are made into farmland.

It will be a long uphill struggle, but the great range of attractive animal species will make tourism more and more important. Savannas are some of the world's last remaining wild places. Increasing numbers of people want to experience this sense of nature, and in doing so they will add the pressure that is needed to care for the environment.

This savanna still has its acacia trees and tall grasses. But there is too much pressure to allow the trees to seed and regenerate, so in time, as the older trees die, there will be no young trees to take their place, and the savanna will lose all its trees.

The most threatened animals are those which have limited defences, have specialized feeding requirements, or which use large areas of land. The ostrich is a bird which is easily caught and its eggs readily stolen.

The key to animal survival in the savannas is the provision of water. Both rivers and natural water holes are gathering grounds for all kinds of animals. Traditionally it has been a dangerous place for the herbivores because predators might lie in wait. But now it is a dangerous place for all because people are a far more serious enemy. These elephants are safely drinking from a water hole in view of a game park lodge. Elsewhere these beautiful elephants would be in danger of being shot for the ivory in their tusks.

GLOSSARY

acacia
a name given to a flat-crowned group of trees that are native to savanna regions. There are many varieties of acacia, but most have long thorns and small leaves

aquifer
a rock which has spaces within it which can store considerable amounts of water and which can be used by people for drinking or irrigation. Groundwater may be the only safe source of drinking water in many parts of the savannas

arid region
a region which has an unpredictable, low rainfall. Arid regions cannot grow crops without irrigation

browsers
herbivores, such as giraffe, that specialize in eating leaves from bushes and trees

carnivores
animals, such as lions, that depend on eating meat to survive

decomposers
animals, such as earthworms and termites, and plants, such as fungi, that eat dead tissue and return nutrients to the soil

food chain
the sequence of plants and animals that depend on each other within an ecosystem. A food chain often contains the following: plants, herbivores, carnivores and decomposers

herbivores
animals, such as zebra, that get their food and energy by eating plants

hibernation
a state of low activity which some animals use as a way of surviving through a period of harsh weather

humid region
a region in which rain falls throughout the year and where there is always substantial moisture in the air

monsoon
a name for the main wet season in some areas bordering the Tropics. A monsoon differs from a normal wet season only in that the rains begin suddenly with torrential downpours

prairie
a region of cool temperate grassland which is too dry for trees to dominate. Wetter parts of a prairie may have trees in them, but when the trees close over to form a continuous canopy, prairie changes to woodland

predator
an animal that hunts other animals for its food

savanna
a tropical region of grass and scattered trees

shifting cultivation
a system of agriculture that people use whereby soil is left fallow, or abandoned, for many years after it has been used for several harvests. The purpose is to let nature rebuild the soil fertility before the land is used for crops again

INDEX